EMMANUEL JOSEPH

The Flow Framework, Designing Days of Productivity, Presence, and Purposeful Relationships

Copyright © 2025 by Emmanuel Joseph

All rights reserved. No part of this publication may be reproduced, stored or transmitted in any form or by any means, electronic, mechanical, photocopying, recording, scanning, or otherwise without written permission from the publisher. It is illegal to copy this book, post it to a website, or distribute it by any other means without permission.

First edition

This book was professionally typeset on Reedsy. Find out more at reedsy.com

Contents

1	Chapter 1: Introduction to the Flow Framework	1
2	Chapter 2: Understanding Flow	3
3	Chapter 3: Designing Your Day	5
4	Chapter 4: Prioritization and Goal Setting	7
5	Chapter 5: Building Positive Habits	9
6	Chapter 6: Mindfulness and Presence	11
7	Chapter 7: The Power of Focus	13
8	Chapter 8: Embracing Flexibility	15
9	Chapter 9: Cultivating Purposeful Relationships	17
10	Chapter 10: Embracing Change	19
11	Chapter 11: Enhancing Creativity	21
12	Chapter 12: Managing Stress	23
13	Chapter 13: Leveraging Technology	25
14	Chapter 14: The Importance of Rest and Recovery	27
15	Chapter 15: The Role of Gratitude	29
16	Chapter 16: Continuous Learning and Growth	31
17	Chapter 17: Living with Intention	33

1

Chapter 1: Introduction to the Flow Framework

In a world that never stops moving, productivity, presence, and purposeful relationships often feel like distant dreams rather than achievable realities. The Flow Framework is born out of the need to find harmony in the chaos of modern life. It is a comprehensive approach designed to help individuals streamline their days, ensuring that every moment is both productive and meaningful. Through the course of this book, we will explore actionable strategies to cultivate a lifestyle that embraces efficiency without sacrificing the joy of being present and the depth of our connections.

The Flow Framework is built on the principle that productivity and presence are not mutually exclusive. By integrating mindful practices with effective time management techniques, we can create a life that is both fulfilling and impactful. Whether you are a professional seeking to enhance your performance, a parent striving to balance work and family, or an individual yearning for deeper connections, this framework offers a path to achieve your goals. The key lies in understanding that every moment matters and that intentionality is the cornerstone of a life well-lived.

In this book, we will embark on a journey to uncover the secrets of the Flow Framework. We will delve into topics such as prioritization, habit formation, and the power of mindfulness. We will explore how to design daily routines that foster creativity, boost productivity, and enhance our ability to be present in every interaction. By the end of our journey, you will have a toolkit of strategies to navigate the complexities of life with grace and purpose. The Flow Framework is not just a method; it is a mindset that empowers you to take control of your life and create meaningful, lasting change.

As we begin this exploration, it is essential to recognize that the Flow Framework is not a one-size-fits-all solution. Each individual's journey is unique, and the framework is designed to be adaptable to your specific needs and circumstances. The principles and practices outlined in this book are meant to serve as a guide, offering insights and techniques that you can tailor to your own life. Embrace this journey with an open mind and a willingness to experiment. The Flow Framework is a powerful tool, but its true strength lies in your commitment to applying its principles consistently and with intention.

2

Chapter 2: Understanding Flow

The concept of "flow" was introduced by psychologist Mihály Csíkszentmihályi, describing a state of optimal experience where individuals are fully immersed in an activity. In the Flow Framework, we build upon this idea to create a holistic approach to life. Flow is not just about peak performance; it is about being fully present and engaged in whatever we do. Achieving flow requires a balance between challenge and skill, where tasks are neither too easy nor too difficult. This chapter delves into the psychology of flow and how it can be harnessed to enhance both productivity and presence.

Flow is characterized by a sense of effortless involvement, where time seems to fly, and self-consciousness fades away. It is in these moments that we produce our best work and experience true joy. However, achieving flow is not accidental; it requires intentionality and practice. We will explore techniques to identify and cultivate flow-inducing activities. By understanding what triggers flow for you, you can design your days to include more of these peak experiences, leading to greater satisfaction and achievement.

The barriers to flow are often internal, such as distractions, stress, and lack of focus. Overcoming these obstacles is crucial to creating an environment conducive to flow. We will discuss strategies to minimize interruptions, manage stress, and enhance concentration. By creating a flow-friendly environment, you can increase your ability to enter and sustain this optimal state. Additionally, we will explore the role of goals and feedback in facilitating flow, helping you set clear objectives and track your progress effectively.

Flow is not limited to work or productivity; it can be experienced in various aspects of life, including hobbies, relationships, and self-care. The Flow Framework encourages a holistic approach, recognizing that balance and fulfillment come from nurturing all areas of life. By integrating flow principles into your daily routines, you can create a life that is rich in meaning and joy. This chapter sets the foundation for the rest of the book, providing the theoretical underpinnings of the Flow Framework and offering practical insights to help you begin your journey towards a more fulfilling life.

3

Chapter 3: Designing Your Day

A well-designed day is the cornerstone of the Flow Framework. It involves a deliberate approach to structuring your time and activities to maximize productivity, presence, and fulfillment. In this chapter, we will explore the principles of effective time management, focusing on prioritization and balance. By taking control of your schedule, you can ensure that your days are aligned with your goals and values. We will introduce the concept of time blocking and how it can be used to create a balanced and productive routine.

Time blocking involves dividing your day into distinct blocks of time, each dedicated to a specific activity or task. This method helps to reduce multitasking and increase focus, allowing you to fully immerse yourself in each activity. We will discuss how to identify your most important tasks and allocate time for them, as well as how to incorporate breaks and leisure activities to prevent burnout. By designing your day with intention, you can create a sense of structure and purpose that supports your overall well-being.

Morning routines play a crucial role in setting the tone for the rest of the day. A mindful and intentional start can boost your energy, focus, and motivation. We will explore various morning routines and how to customize them to suit your preferences and goals. From meditation and exercise to journaling and goal-setting, we will provide practical tips to help you craft a morning routine that sets you up for success. Additionally, we will discuss the importance of evening routines in winding down and preparing for restful sleep.

Flexibility is an essential aspect of the Flow Framework. While structure is important, it is equally important to remain adaptable and responsive to changing circumstances. We will discuss strategies for maintaining flexibility within your daily routine, allowing you to pivot and adjust as needed. By embracing a balanced approach to structure and flexibility, you can create a dynamic and resilient daily routine that supports your productivity, presence, and overall well-being. This chapter provides practical tools and insights to help you design your day with intention and purpose.

4

Chapter 4: Prioritization and Goal Setting

Effective prioritization and goal setting are fundamental to the Flow Framework. They enable you to focus your efforts on what truly matters, ensuring that your actions are aligned with your long-term aspirations. In this chapter, we will explore various techniques for setting meaningful goals and prioritizing tasks. By understanding the difference between urgent and important tasks, you can make informed decisions about where to invest your time and energy.

One of the most powerful tools for prioritization is the Eisenhower Matrix, which categorizes tasks into four quadrants based on their urgency and importance. We will discuss how to use this matrix to identify high-priority tasks and eliminate or delegate low-priority ones. Additionally, we will explore the concept of "Big Rocks," which involves focusing on the most significant and impactful tasks before attending to smaller, less critical ones. By prioritizing effectively, you can ensure that your efforts are directed towards activities that contribute to your long-term goals and values.

Goal setting is a dynamic and iterative process that requires regular reflection and adjustment. We will discuss the importance of setting SMART goals—Specific, Measurable, Achievable, Relevant, and Time-bound—and how to break them down into actionable steps. By creating a clear roadmap for your goals, you can track your progress and stay motivated. We will also explore the role of accountability and support in achieving your goals, emphasizing the value of seeking feedback and collaboration.

In addition to setting long-term goals, it is important to establish short-term milestones that provide a sense of accomplishment and momentum. We will discuss techniques for setting daily and weekly goals that align with your broader objectives. By celebrating small wins and regularly reviewing your progress, you can maintain a positive and motivated mindset. This chapter provides practical strategies for prioritization and goal setting, empowering you to take intentional action towards a fulfilling and purpose-driven life.

5

Chapter 5: Building Positive Habits

Habits are the building blocks of our daily routines and play a crucial role in shaping our lives. In this chapter, we will explore the science of habit formation and how to build positive habits that support the Flow Framework. Habits are powerful because they automate behaviors, reducing the need for conscious effort and decision-making. By understanding the mechanics of habits, we can intentionally design our routines to include behaviors that enhance productivity, presence, and purpose.

The habit loop, consisting of a cue, routine, and reward, is a fundamental concept in habit formation. We will discuss how to identify cues that trigger desired behaviors and how to create routines that are enjoyable and sustainable. By linking positive habits to immediate rewards, we can reinforce and strengthen them over time. Additionally, we will explore strategies for breaking bad habits and replacing them with more constructive ones. Understanding the habit loop empowers us to take control of our behaviors and create lasting change.

Consistency is key to building positive habits. We will discuss techniques for maintaining consistency, such as setting specific goals, tracking progress, and celebrating small wins. The concept of "habit stacking" involves linking new habits to existing ones, making it easier to integrate them into our daily routines. By leveraging the power of existing habits, we can build new ones more effectively. We will also explore the role of accountability and support in sustaining positive habits, emphasizing the importance of community and collaboration.

Habits are not just about individual behaviors; they also influence our relationships and interactions with others. We will discuss how to cultivate habits that enhance our connections with others, such as active listening, expressing gratitude, and practicing empathy. By building positive relational habits, we can create deeper and more meaningful relationships. This chapter provides practical insights and strategies for building positive habits that support the Flow Framework and contribute to a fulfilling and purpose-driven life.

6

Chapter 6: Mindfulness and Presence

Mindfulness is the practice of being fully present and engaged in the current moment. It is a powerful tool for enhancing both productivity and presence, as it allows us to focus our attention and reduce distractions. In this chapter, we will explore the principles of mindfulness and how to integrate them into our daily routines. By cultivating mindfulness, we can increase our ability to enter a state of flow and create more meaningful and intentional interactions.

Mindfulness involves paying attention to our thoughts, emotions, and sensations without judgment. We will discuss various mindfulness techniques, such as meditation, deep breathing, and body scans, and how to incorporate them into our daily routines. These practices help to reduce stress, enhance focus, and improve overall well-being. By starting with small, manageable mindfulness practices, we can gradually build a more mindful and present lifestyle.

The benefits of mindfulness extend beyond individual well-being; they also enhance our relationships and interactions with others. We will explore how to practice mindful communication, active listening, and empathy. By being fully present in our interactions, we can create deeper connections and foster more meaningful relationships. Mindfulness also helps us to manage conflict and respond to challenges with greater resilience and compassion.

Mindfulness is not just a practice; it is a mindset that influences all aspects of our lives. We will discuss how to cultivate a mindful mindset and integrate mindfulness into our daily activities, such as eating, working, and exercising. By approaching each moment with intention and presence, we can create a life that is rich in meaning and fulfillment. This chapter provides practical tools and insights to help you cultivate mindfulness and enhance your ability to be present in every aspect of your life.

7

Chapter 7: The Power of Focus

Focus is the ability to direct our attention and energy towards a specific task or goal. It is a critical component of the Flow Framework, as it enables us to achieve deep work and enter a state of flow. In this chapter, we will explore the principles of focus and how to cultivate it in our daily routines. By enhancing our ability to focus, we can increase our productivity, reduce distractions, and create more meaningful and impactful work.

Distractions are one of the biggest barriers to focus. We will discuss strategies for minimizing distractions, such as creating a conducive work environment, setting boundaries, and managing digital interruptions. By identifying and eliminating common sources of distraction, we can create a focused and productive workspace. Additionally, we will explore techniques for managing internal distractions, such as intrusive thoughts and stress, and how to maintain focus in challenging situations.

Deep work is a state of focused and uninterrupted work that allows us to produce high-quality and impactful results. We will discuss the principles of deep work and how to create conditions that support it. Techniques such as time blocking, batching similar tasks, and using the Pomodoro Technique can help to enhance focus and productivity. By dedicating time and energy to deep work, we can achieve greater levels of creativity, problem-solving, and performance.

Focus is not just about work; it also influences our ability to be present in our relationships and interactions. We will explore how to practice focused and intentional communication, active listening, and empathy. By being fully present in our interactions, we can create deeper and more meaningful connections with others. This chapter provides practical insights and strategies for cultivating focus and enhancing our ability to achieve deep work and meaningful presence.

8

Chapter 8: Embracing Flexibility

Flexibility is an essential aspect of the Flow Framework, as it allows us to adapt to changing circumstances and respond to unexpected challenges. In this chapter, we will explore the principles of flexibility and how to integrate them into our daily routines. By embracing flexibility, we can create a dynamic and resilient lifestyle that supports our productivity, presence, and overall well-being.

Flexibility involves being open to change and willing to adjust our plans and routines as needed. We will discuss strategies for cultivating a flexible mindset, such as practicing mindfulness, setting realistic expectations, and embracing uncertainty. By approaching each day with a sense of curiosity and openness, we can navigate the complexities of life with greater ease and resilience.

Flexibility also involves creating adaptable routines and structures that can accommodate changing priorities and circumstances. We will explore techniques for maintaining flexibility within our daily schedules, such as time blocking, setting buffer times, and prioritizing tasks. By building flexibility into our routines, we can create a balanced and adaptable approach to productivity and presence.

Flexibility is not just about individual behaviors; it also influences our relationships and interactions with others. We will discuss how to practice flexible and adaptive communication, active listening, and empathy. By being open to different perspectives and willing to adjust our interactions, we can create deeper and more meaningful connections with others. This chapter provides practical insights and strategies for embracing flexibility and creating a dynamic and resilient lifestyle that supports the Flow Framework.

9

Chapter 9: Cultivating Purposeful Relationships

Purposeful relationships are a cornerstone of a fulfilling life. They provide support, joy, and a sense of belonging. In this chapter, we will explore the principles of building and nurturing purposeful relationships. By focusing on intentional communication, empathy, and mutual respect, we can create deeper and more meaningful connections with others. The Flow Framework emphasizes the importance of investing time and energy into our relationships to enhance our overall well-being.

Effective communication is the foundation of any strong relationship. We will discuss techniques for improving communication, such as active listening, clear expression, and non-verbal cues. By practicing mindful communication, we can reduce misunderstandings and foster a greater sense of connection. Additionally, we will explore the role of empathy in relationships, emphasizing the importance of understanding and validating the feelings and perspectives of others.

Building purposeful relationships also involves setting healthy boundaries and managing conflicts constructively. We will discuss strategies for establishing and maintaining boundaries that respect both our needs and the needs of others. By addressing conflicts with empathy and a solution-oriented mindset, we can strengthen our relationships and create a more harmonious environment. We will also explore the importance of forgiveness and how it can facilitate healing and growth in our relationships.

Purposeful relationships are not limited to romantic or family connections; they also include friendships, professional relationships, and community ties. We will discuss how to cultivate meaningful connections in various contexts, from networking in professional settings to building a sense of community in our neighborhoods. By investing in purposeful relationships, we can create a support system that enhances our overall well-being and enriches our lives.

10

Chapter 10: Embracing Change

Change is an inevitable part of life, and our ability to embrace it significantly impacts our overall well-being and success. In this chapter, we will explore the principles of embracing change and how to navigate transitions with grace and resilience. The Flow Framework emphasizes the importance of adaptability and a growth mindset in responding to change. By approaching change with a positive and proactive attitude, we can turn challenges into opportunities for growth and development.

Change often brings uncertainty and discomfort, but it also presents opportunities for learning and growth. We will discuss strategies for managing the emotions and stress associated with change, such as practicing mindfulness, seeking support, and focusing on the positive aspects of the transition. By developing a resilient mindset, we can navigate change more effectively and emerge stronger and more capable.

Adaptability is a key skill for embracing change. We will explore techniques for enhancing adaptability, such as staying open to new experiences, being flexible in our thinking, and continuously learning and growing. By cultivating adaptability, we can respond to change with greater ease and confidence. Additionally, we will discuss the importance of setting realistic expectations and being patient with ourselves as we navigate transitions.

Embracing change also involves taking proactive steps to shape our future. We will discuss how to set goals and take intentional actions that align with our long-term aspirations. By approaching change with a sense of purpose and direction, we can create a more fulfilling and meaningful life. This chapter provides practical insights and strategies for embracing change and navigating transitions with resilience and grace.

11

Chapter 11: Enhancing Creativity

Creativity is a vital component of the Flow Framework, as it enhances our ability to problem-solve, innovate, and express ourselves. In this chapter, we will explore the principles of enhancing creativity and how to integrate creative practices into our daily routines. By cultivating a creative mindset, we can approach challenges with curiosity and open-mindedness, leading to more innovative and effective solutions.

Creativity is not limited to artistic endeavors; it can be applied to various aspects of life, from work and relationships to hobbies and self-care. We will discuss techniques for enhancing creativity, such as brainstorming, mind mapping, and seeking diverse perspectives. By embracing a playful and experimental approach, we can unlock our creative potential and discover new possibilities.

The environment plays a significant role in fostering creativity. We will explore how to create a conducive environment for creativity, such as organizing our workspace, reducing distractions, and incorporating elements that inspire us. Additionally, we will discuss the importance of taking breaks and allowing our minds to wander, as these moments of rest can often lead to creative insights and breakthroughs.

Creativity is a skill that can be developed and nurtured over time. We will discuss the importance of practice and persistence in enhancing our creative abilities. By engaging in regular creative activities and challenging ourselves to think outside the box, we can continuously grow and evolve. This chapter provides practical tools and insights to help you enhance your creativity and integrate it into your daily life.

12

Chapter 12: Managing Stress

Stress is a common experience in modern life, and effectively managing it is essential for our overall well-being and productivity. In this chapter, we will explore the principles of stress management and how to incorporate stress-reducing practices into our daily routines. The Flow Framework emphasizes the importance of addressing stress proactively and creating a balanced and resilient lifestyle.

Understanding the sources of stress is the first step in managing it. We will discuss common stressors, such as work demands, relationships, and personal expectations, and how to identify and address them. By recognizing the underlying causes of stress, we can take targeted actions to reduce its impact on our lives.

There are various techniques for managing stress, ranging from mindfulness practices to physical activities. We will explore strategies such as meditation, deep breathing, exercise, and time management. By incorporating these practices into our daily routines, we can reduce stress and enhance our overall well-being. Additionally, we will discuss the importance of self-care and setting boundaries to prevent burnout.

Resilience is a crucial aspect of stress management. We will discuss how to build resilience by cultivating a positive mindset, seeking support, and embracing challenges as opportunities for growth. By developing resilience, we can navigate stress more effectively and maintain our well-being in the face of adversity. This chapter provides practical insights and strategies for managing stress and creating a balanced and resilient lifestyle.

13

Chapter 13: Leveraging Technology

In today's digital age, technology plays a significant role in shaping our productivity and presence. In this chapter, we will explore how to leverage technology effectively to support the Flow Framework. While technology can be a powerful tool for enhancing efficiency and connectivity, it can also be a source of distraction and stress. By understanding how to use technology mindfully, we can harness its benefits without compromising our well-being.

There are numerous tools and apps designed to enhance productivity, such as task managers, calendar apps, and time-tracking software. We will discuss how to choose the right tools for your needs and integrate them into your daily routines. By using technology to streamline tasks and manage time effectively, we can free up mental space and focus on more meaningful activities. Additionally, we will explore techniques for minimizing digital distractions and maintaining a healthy balance between screen time and offline activities.

Technology also offers opportunities for enhancing communication and collaboration. We will discuss how to use digital platforms to build and maintain purposeful relationships, both personally and professionally. By leveraging technology for virtual meetings, online communities, and social networking, we can stay connected and engaged with others. However, it is essential to practice mindful communication and set boundaries to prevent digital fatigue and maintain meaningful interactions.

Mindful use of technology involves being intentional about when and how we engage with digital devices. We will explore strategies for creating tech-free zones and times, such as designated digital detox periods and screen-free spaces. By setting boundaries and practicing digital mindfulness, we can reduce the negative impact of technology on our well-being and enhance our ability to be present in the moment. This chapter provides practical insights and strategies for leveraging technology to support the Flow Framework and create a balanced and purposeful life.

14

Chapter 14: The Importance of Rest and Recovery

Rest and recovery are essential components of the Flow Framework, as they allow us to recharge and maintain our overall well-being. In this chapter, we will explore the principles of rest and recovery and how to incorporate them into our daily routines. By prioritizing rest and recovery, we can enhance our productivity, presence, and overall quality of life.

Sleep is a crucial aspect of rest and recovery. We will discuss the importance of getting adequate sleep and how to improve sleep quality. Techniques such as establishing a consistent sleep schedule, creating a relaxing bedtime routine, and optimizing the sleep environment can help to enhance sleep quality. Additionally, we will explore the impact of diet, exercise, and stress management on sleep, and how to create a holistic approach to rest and recovery.

Rest is not limited to sleep; it also includes activities that promote relaxation and rejuvenation. We will discuss various forms of rest, such as physical rest, mental rest, and emotional rest, and how to incorporate them into our daily routines. Techniques such as meditation, deep breathing, and mindfulness can help to promote relaxation and reduce stress. By prioritizing rest and recovery, we can maintain our energy levels and enhance our ability to be present and productive.

Recovery is the process of restoring our physical, mental, and emotional well-being after periods of exertion or stress. We will explore strategies for effective recovery, such as active recovery, self-care practices, and seeking support from others. By creating a balanced approach to rest and recovery, we can enhance our resilience and overall well-being. This chapter provides practical insights and strategies for prioritizing rest and recovery and integrating them into the Flow Framework.

15

Chapter 15: The Role of Gratitude

Gratitude is a powerful practice that enhances our overall well-being and supports the Flow Framework. In this chapter, we will explore the principles of gratitude and how to incorporate them into our daily routines. By practicing gratitude, we can shift our focus from what is lacking to what we have, leading to greater contentment and fulfillment.

Gratitude involves recognizing and appreciating the positive aspects of our lives. We will discuss various gratitude practices, such as keeping a gratitude journal, expressing gratitude to others, and practicing mindfulness. By regularly reflecting on the things we are grateful for, we can cultivate a more positive and optimistic mindset. Additionally, we will explore the science of gratitude and how it impacts our mental and emotional well-being.

Gratitude also enhances our relationships and interactions with others. We will discuss how to express gratitude in our relationships, such as through acts of kindness, verbal acknowledgments, and thoughtful gestures. By practicing gratitude in our interactions, we can create deeper and more meaningful connections with others. Additionally, we will explore how to cultivate a culture of gratitude in our communities and workplaces, fostering a positive and supportive environment.

The practice of gratitude is not limited to moments of joy and success; it can also be applied during challenging times. We will discuss how to find silver linings and practice gratitude even in difficult situations. By embracing a gratitude mindset, we can build resilience and maintain a sense of hope and optimism. This chapter provides practical insights and strategies for cultivating gratitude and integrating it into the Flow Framework to enhance our overall well-being and fulfillment.

16

Chapter 16: Continuous Learning and Growth

Continuous learning and growth are essential components of the Flow Framework, as they enable us to evolve and adapt in an ever-changing world. In this chapter, we will explore the principles of continuous learning and how to cultivate a growth mindset. By embracing a commitment to lifelong learning, we can enhance our skills, knowledge, and overall well-being.

A growth mindset involves believing that our abilities and intelligence can be developed through effort and practice. We will discuss techniques for cultivating a growth mindset, such as embracing challenges, seeking feedback, and viewing failures as opportunities for learning. By adopting a growth mindset, we can approach life with curiosity and resilience, continuously striving to improve and evolve.

There are various ways to engage in continuous learning, such as formal education, self-directed learning, and experiential learning. We will explore different learning modalities and how to integrate them into our daily routines. By setting learning goals and seeking diverse experiences, we can expand our horizons and enhance our personal and professional development. Additionally, we will discuss the importance of reflection and how to use it as a tool for continuous improvement.

Continuous learning is not just about acquiring new knowledge; it also involves cultivating wisdom and self-awareness. We will discuss how to develop self-awareness through practices such as journaling, meditation, and seeking feedback. By deepening our understanding of ourselves, we can make more informed decisions and align our actions with our values and goals. This chapter provides practical insights and strategies for embracing continuous learning and growth and integrating them into the Flow Framework.

17

Chapter 17: Living with Intention

Living with intention is the culmination of the Flow Framework, as it involves making conscious and deliberate choices that align with our values and goals. In this final chapter, we will explore the principles of intentional living and how to integrate them into our daily routines. By living with intention, we can create a life that is rich in meaning and fulfillment.

Intentional living involves being clear about our values and priorities and making decisions that reflect them. We will discuss techniques for identifying and clarifying our values, such as self-reflection, journaling, and seeking feedback. By understanding what truly matters to us, we can make choices that are aligned with our long-term aspirations and create a sense of purpose and direction.

Intentional living also involves being present and mindful in each moment. We will explore how to practice mindfulness and presence in our daily activities, such as through meditation, deep breathing, and mindful communication. By being fully engaged in each moment, we can create deeper and more meaningful experiences and connections. Additionally, we will discuss the importance of setting goals and taking intentional actions that align with our values and priorities.

The journey of living with intention is ongoing and requires regular reflection and adjustment. We will discuss the importance of regular self-assessment and how to make course corrections as needed. By continuously evaluating our actions and choices, we can ensure that we are living in alignment with our values and goals. This final chapter provides practical insights and strategies for living with intention and integrating the Flow Framework into every aspect of our lives.

The Flow Framework: Designing Days of Productivity, Presence, and Purposeful Relationships

In a fast-paced world where time seems to slip away, achieving a balance between productivity, presence, and meaningful relationships often feels unattainable. "The Flow Framework" offers a comprehensive approach to reclaiming that balance and creating a life that is both efficient and fulfilling. Through this insightful book, readers will discover actionable strategies to streamline their days and embrace a lifestyle that integrates mindfulness with effective time management.

The Flow Framework is grounded in the principle that productivity and presence can coexist harmoniously. By adopting mindful practices and setting intentional routines, individuals can enhance their performance while staying connected to the present moment. This book delves into a wide range of topics, including habit formation, goal setting, and the power of mindfulness, to help readers design their days with purpose and clarity.

With practical tools and relatable examples, "The Flow Framework" guides readers on a journey towards a more intentional and balanced life. It emphasizes the importance of cultivating positive habits, managing stress, and embracing change with resilience. Readers will learn how to build deeper, more meaningful relationships and leverage technology mindfully to support their goals.

Whether you are a professional striving for peak performance, a parent seeking balance between work and family, or an individual longing for deeper connections, this book provides a customizable toolkit to navigate life's complexities with grace. "The Flow Framework" is not just a method; it is a mindset that empowers readers to take control of their lives and create lasting, positive change.

Join us on this journey to design days filled with productivity, presence, and purposeful relationships. Embrace the Flow Framework and unlock the potential for a life well-lived.

www.ingramcontent.com/pod-product-compliance
Lightning Source LLC
LaVergne TN
LVHW020458080526
838202LV00057B/6035